Asher Taylor

Notes of Conversations with a Volunteer Officer in the United States Navy,

on the passage of the forts below New Orleans, April 24th, 1862, and

other points of service on the Mississippi River during that year

Asher Taylor

Notes of Conversations with a Volunteer Officer in the United States Navy,
*on the passage of the forts below New Orleans, April 24th, 1862, and other points
of service on the Mississippi River during that year*

ISBN/EAN: 9783337377175

Printed in Europe, USA, Canada, Australia, Japan

Cover: Foto ©ninafisch / pixelio.de

More available books at **www.hansebooks.com**

THE GREAT REBELLION.

"Gather up the fragments that nothing be lost."

CAPTAIN GORHAM COFFIN TAYLOR, of the City of New York, received the appointment of Volunteer Master's Mate in the U. S. Navy, in the forepart of November, 1861. He immediately proceeded, under orders, to Washington, and reported at the Navy Yard there, and was placed, together with a number of others—Captains, Mates and Second Mates, volunteers from the merchant service—under instruction in the peculiar duties of the navy—

"The lore of the bold and the brave."

An experience of ten years at sea as boy, seaman, mate and captain, had given him all the qualification in practical seamanship, and sailor-craft generally, that could be desired. In December he was ordered to Philadelphia, and attached to the *Sciota*, gun-boat.

The United States gunboat *Sciota*, a steamer, schooner rigged, of five hundred tons burthen, was a formid-

able vessel of her class, carrying a 20-pounder Parrott rifle on her top-gallant forecastle; an XI-inch Dahlgren on a pivot amidship, and two 24-pounder brass howitzers on her quarters; a third howitzer was added after her arrival in the "Gulf." She was built and fitted away at Philadelphia; whence she sailed on the 17th of December, 1861, under command of Lieut.-Com'g ED-WARD DONALDSON, the oldest lieutenant in the navy, to join the "Western Gulf Squadron" at its rendezvous at Ship Island, in the Gulf of Mexico; she arrived out on the 8th January, 1862.

In a short time Captain DAVID G. FARRAGUT hoisted his "Flag" as Commander-in-Chief of the naval forces destined for the reduction of New Orleans, and the opening of the Mississippi above that point.

Marvelous stories were circulated of the tremendous obstacles to be encountered; mighty iron-clad rams of novel construction, and other vessels of great power, vauntingly proclaimed by the "Rebs" and their friends to be impregnable and irresistible; Fort Jackson, on the west side of the river, mounting nearly a hundred guns of most formidable character;

Fort St. Philip, opposite ; and, in addition, an enormous chain stretched across the river, borne on hulks, at a point to obstruct the passage, under the guns of the Fort ; all combining to present a resistance appearing to many as impossible to be overcome by any forces that the Government would be able to present against it.

By the forepart of April the *Sciota*, with most of the vessels of Flag-officer FARRAGUT's Squadron, had entered the river, and were lying at the "head of the passes," whilst the last touches of preparation for the approaching great conflict were given ; amongst which, the trifling incident of the *Sciota* being sent out to Isle au Breton, one of the sand keys just outside of the river, conveying a schooner for a load of beach sand, to strew on the decks of the vessels in action, to prevent them from being splashy and slippery with blood, was rather suggestive, the boys, who had never been in action, thought, of the "raw-head and bloody-bones" kind of work before them.

Whilst the attack on the forts was impending, the fleet was visited by the commanders and other officers of the English and French war vessels lying in the river, and who had been up to the city and observed the measures for defence ; and it was stated that they were all very emphatic in expressing their opinions that the attempt to silence or pass the forts must prove a failure, involving the defeat and probable destruction of the fleet. Doubtless "the wish was father to the thought," for old Cockney Johnny, the old thief, and Johnny Crapeau, too— "and be cursed to them !"—were both openly in sympathy and fraternity with the *Johnny Rebs*.

The MORTAR FLEET, of twenty vessels, took positions at ranges of a mile and a half to over two miles (2650 to 3680 yards) from the Forts, and in due time opened on them, and kept up a continual fire for five or six days and nights, with effects that have never been surpassed, if equalled, in any former or modern gunnery.

The *Sciota*, with the Flag-officer and a number of other *big wigs*, including the General commanding the co-operating military force, and some of the principal wise ones of his staff, on board, was several times pushed up, scouting, toward the forts to reconnoitre, and see how things looked, and draw their fire, to judge of the powers and range of their artillery. The boys were not a little amused at the effects on the different members of the quarter-deck party, of the approach of an occasional well-directed shot from Johnny Reb; whilst the old bull-dog, the Flag-officer, with glass in hand, stood on the horse-block, bolt upright, staunch and immovable as the stump of the mainmast, with a—"There comes one!—there!!—*there!!!*" And, as the shot fell into the water, "Ah, too short; finely lined, tho'!"—the doughty General, and the *greeneys* of his "*tail*," ducked and bobbed, and dodged in a manner to greatly excite the merriment of the "blue jackets" forward. Sailors have, generally, a quick eye for the ridiculous, in whatever passes within their notice, especially with those ranking over them.

The Rebs were very active in the employment of every means of annoyance—sending down, almost nightly, fire hulks and immense rafts piled up with blazing combustibles, which kept the whole fleet on the alert in fighting them off. One night a very formidable raft was coming down, and a gun-boat, just ahead of the *Sciota*, hove up her anchor to run clear of it, the current, getting a sheer on her, carried her down on to the *Sciota*, and started *her* anchors, and the two fell athwart the hawse of one of the frigates (the *Mississippi*) when the raft struck them, and caused, for a few moments, much excitement in all three of the vessels. They succeeded, however, by great exertions, in shoving it off, with some damage by fire to the head-gear of the *Sciota;* and before she could get disentangled and out of the scrape, she lost her mainmast. Her foremast was subsequently knocked out of her in one of her engagements up the river, and she performed her work, during the latter part of the summer, entirely *bare of poles*.

The formidable rebel chain was most gallantly and adroitly unshackled or cut, under the cover of night, and an opening made in it sufficient for the vessels to pass through, previous to the movement of the fleet up to the attack.

All things being in readiness, and the "bomb fleet" having been for several days incessantly "pumping thunder" into the devoted forts, the morning of the 24th of April had been appointed for the decisive movement; and accordingly, all hands were turned up, at the appearance of the Flag-officer's "two red lights" just after midnight, responding to the summons on board our ship, and, in fact, throughout the fleet, with great spirit and alacrity, all in high glee and eager for the fray.

The morning was dark; a heavy damp mist hung over the

water. Some two or three hours were spent in "backing and filling"—yawiug about—getting the vessels into their respective positions. After the first excitement of the "rattle up" was over—time hanging heavy with them—TAYLOR and another steerage officer went below and played *dominoes* for pastime (that being the highest grade of "sport" allowed in a man-of-war), until "all hands to quarters" was called, when, stretching their limbs, and shaking off their languor, they buckled on their swords, with revolvers on the belts, and rushed to the deck and took position at their several divisions: young WOODWARD, an embryo Acting Middy, having the rifle on the forecastle; FOSTER, Acting Master, the XI-inch Dahlgren amidships; TAYLOR, the *three* howitzers on the quarters; and McFARLAND, Sailing Master, at the *con.*

The fleet moved off gallantly, in two lines, up to the work—the *Sciota*, being No. 1 of the gunboats, leading the second division of gunboats, in support of the first division of ships (the port column), led by the Commander-in-Chief in the *Hartford.*＊ Large fires were built on the shores by the Rebs, to light up the river and expose the vessels to view from the forts and batteries, and as they came within range they were opened upon with a tremendous cannonade. Meanwhile, the bomb vessels kept pouring into the forts a perfect torrent of their terrific missiles; TAYLOR counted thirteen shells in the air at one time, all speeding, screaming, at the devoted objects of the attack. The river was full of rebel vessels—gunboats, fire-ships and fire-rafts drifting down, giving the appearance of a sea of flame, into the midst of which the fleet was pushing, and, altogether,

＊ "The dear old *Hartford!*"—Mrs. FARRAGUT.

presenting a scene awfully terrible, and grand beyond description.

Captain PORTER, commanding the Mortar Fleet, in a dispatch to the Secretary of the Navy, written the next day, before he had heard from above of the result of the movement, remarks:

"The sight of this night attack was awfully grand. The "river was lit up by rafts filled with pine-knots, and the "ships seemed to be literally fighting in an ocean of flame and "smoke.

"I am in hopes the ships above fared as well as we did, "though amid such a terrible fire. It was gratifying to see "that not a ship wavered, but stood steadily on her course; "and I am in hopes (and I see no reason to doubt it) that they "now have possession of New Orleans."

The prescribed order for the movement of the vessels was disregarded after passing through the opening in the chain; each one, as she got through, pushed on at the top of her speed, and engaged the forts and the Reb gunboats as she encountered them. Of the five ships and twelve gunboats composing the fleet, the *Sciota* was the fourth one to attack the forts and pass them; the *Varuna*, and another gunboat (both very fast), and one of the large ships, preceded her. The action soon became general; the *Sciota* opened from her whole batteries, which were served with vigor and spirit, aiming, in the darkness, at the flashes from the forts. TAYLOR took position on the after

hatch (the ward-room sky-light), so as to have a good oversight
of his three guns, two of which were trained to port on Fort
Jackson, and the third to starboard on St. Phillip, and directing and cheering on his men to their utmost efforts of activity.
The fire from the heavy ordnance of the forts was tremendous,
and tremendously was it responded to by the fleet. It was
estimated that the fire from both sides—the fleet, the forts, the
rebel vessels, and the batteries on the shore—numbered six
hundred guns within a square mile, and worked with a rapidity
unparalleled in previous times. Well did Flag-officer FARRA-
GUT say, in his first letter to the Secretary of the Navy, "*Such
a fire, I imagine, the world has rarely seen!*" On the *Sciota*,
every man, although but few of them had ever been under fire,
evinced the utmost unqualified bravery, and to a degree that
was truly remarkable; all was glee and jollity with them—
cheering, shouting, and joking at every incident. And when a
shot would come crashing through the bulwarks, or sides of the
vessel, the inquiry was general, and with deep interest, "Who's
hit?" "Who's hurt?" No one concerned for himself, but all
anxious about their shipmates; in fact, not a man was wanting,
in the slightest degree, in the highest qualification of "a brave
Yankee tar!"

Just after the *Sciota* had passed the front of Fort Jackson,
and still within range of the fire from its heavy guns, a large
rebel armed steamer, the *Resolute*, came near her; and, as
soon as discovered in the darkness and smoke, the *Sciota* was
training her batteries on her, they called out from her, "Don't
fire, for God's sake!—we surrender!" The Fleet Captain, who
commanded a division of the gunboats, was, with his pennant

(his divisional "flag"), on the *Sciota*, and directed the First
Lieutenant to send a boat to board her. A cutter was "Called
away," and TAYLOR—whose position with his Howitzer Division on the quarter-deck, being close to the Lieutenant—hear-
ing the order of the Fleet Captain, turned to the Lieutenant and
asked if he might go in the boat. The *Luff* seemed startled at
the reckless daring of the request, and answered, "Why—a—
yes—if you *wish to!*" TAYLOR ordered the cutter down, and
as he sprang into it, called on his division for volunteers, when
all his men tumbled forward in a moment to the gangway, and
many of them into the boat. He selected six, and sent the
others back to their guns; and with his six "armed up" with
cutlass and revolvers, he pushed off in search of the prize,
which had drifted by, down into the fog and smoke, out of
sight. The fire on all sides was terrific, but they "gave way,
with a will," and after pulling half a mile or more, dodging
about amidst the terrible fire, and through the crowd of vessels,
of both sides, that seemed to fill the river, found their customer,
with his head run into the mud, and aground on the bank of
the river, just above Fort Jackson ; they ran alongside, and
she being high up out of water, and no chain-plates or projec-
tions of any kind to hang on to, it was a problem, for a moment, how to get on board of her; which, however, was soon
solved by several of his men taking TAYLOR by the feet and
raising him square up, and fairly tossing him on to the deck of
the rebel, where a scene of carnage and suffering met his eye,
such as he had never before witnessed. The *Resolute*, just before encountering the *Sciota*, had received smashing broadsides
from one of the large ships as she passed her, which had terribly cut up and almost annihilated her crew ; upwards of a

hundred of them lay in heaps, dead and wounded, and some mangled horribly. Two of TAYLOR's crew followed him to the deck of the rebel, and, pistol in hand, "stood by him." On inquiring for the commanding officer, the Second Lieutenant, who met him at the side of the vessel, informed him that the Captain was up on the boiler-deck, mortally wounded, and that the First Lieutenant was in command; TAYLOR then required to be conducted to the commanding Lieutenant, and proceeded, flanked by his faithful supporters, to the upper deck, where the Lieutenant was in attendance on the dying Captain. As he approached them, the Lieutenant came forward to meet him, and, drawing his sword, tendered it, saying, "*I surrender the ship to you, sir!*" TAYLOR received the sword, and extending his hand to the Lieutenant shook hands with him, and held a few minutes' conversation on the condition of the ship and of the crew. Whilst they stood talking together, a beautiful bright-eyed boy, of some ten or twelve years, approached them; the Lieutenant said he was the Captain's son, called him Eugene, and told him they were all prisoners. TAYLOR, finding the vessel hard aground, and impossible to be moved, turned to the Lieutenant, and the Second Lieutenant, who had joined them, saying, "Gentlemen, you will please get into the boat and go with me, I have no time to spare;" and also told Eugene that he, too, must get into the boat, designing to protect and take care of him amidst the confusion. The little fellow straightened himself up, and replied, "*No, sir!* I will stay with my father; he is wounded, and I am going to stay with him as long as he lives." TAYLOR was surprised and amused at the spirited and saucy air, and yet feeling manner in which he was answered, and told the boy that he was a fine fellow

—"a brick"—and might remain with his father, and must do everything in his power for his comfort.

As they moved forward toward their boat, they had to pick their steps among the dead and dying and wounded; and as he stepped over a poor fellow, terribly mangled, who moaned out, "Oh, for God's sake, give me some water!" TAYLOR called out, with the instinctive tone of authority, "For'ard there!" and receiving from half a dozen the accustomed "Aye, aye, sir," he continued, "Some of you bring some water for this poor fellow, and put something under his head, and lay him more comfortably." The saddened look of gratitude and tenderness that the wounded man turned up to the speaker was inexpressibly touching, and started a tear that subsequent scenes of carnage and suffering have failed to move.

TAYLOR, with his prisoners, the two Lieutenants, then pushed off on his return to his own ship. All this work was done with but six men, and the *Resolute* had, perhaps, fifty or more of her crew remaining unhurt, and was still within range of the forts and under the fire of the rebel vessels, particularly the gunboat *McRea*, which lay abreast, and kept up a sharp and constant fire directed at the boat, but, luckily, the party escaped being hit by any of them.

After getting into the boat, TAYLOR, having the surrendered sword in his hand, suggested that it would be convenient to have the scabbard also, when the Lieutenant unclasped the belt and handed it over, to accompany the sword; remarking afterwards, on board the *Sciota*, that the request, so coolly made when under such a crushing fire, and with such perilous surroundings, showed a degree of "cheek," and freedom from excitement, that was remarkable.

The passage back was, if possible, more perilous than the outset; the fire around them, from the rebel vessels, seemed heavier and closer. The density of the smoke, and the dim gray of the morning, had long shut out from their sight their own vessel; and as they were pulling in the direction of where they expected to find her, they discovered an odd, black, non-descript-looking thing moving out from under the shore directly across their course. TAYLOR could not imagine what it was, but was informed by his prisoners that it was the famous ram *Manassas*. They seemed elated at her near approach and apparent likelihood to intercept and perhaps recapture them; but TAYLOR, not exactly relishing that contingency, altered his course, making a wide detour to avoid her; and, after a long pull, dodging about amongst the vessels, regained his own ship in safety. His Captain, having lost sight of him for so long a time, had given him up as lost—sunk or captured, certain—and had given the order to "go ahead," abandoning him entirely. His Sailing Master, and others, exclaimed against it, reminding him that the boat was still out, when he, apparently rather reluctantly, held on, and in a little while discovered the boat in the distance, under the smoke, and in due time took her up.

TAYLOR was welcomed from his perilous *voyage* with warm congratulations by all on board. On presenting his prisoners to Fleet-Captain BELL, he was complimented by him in the

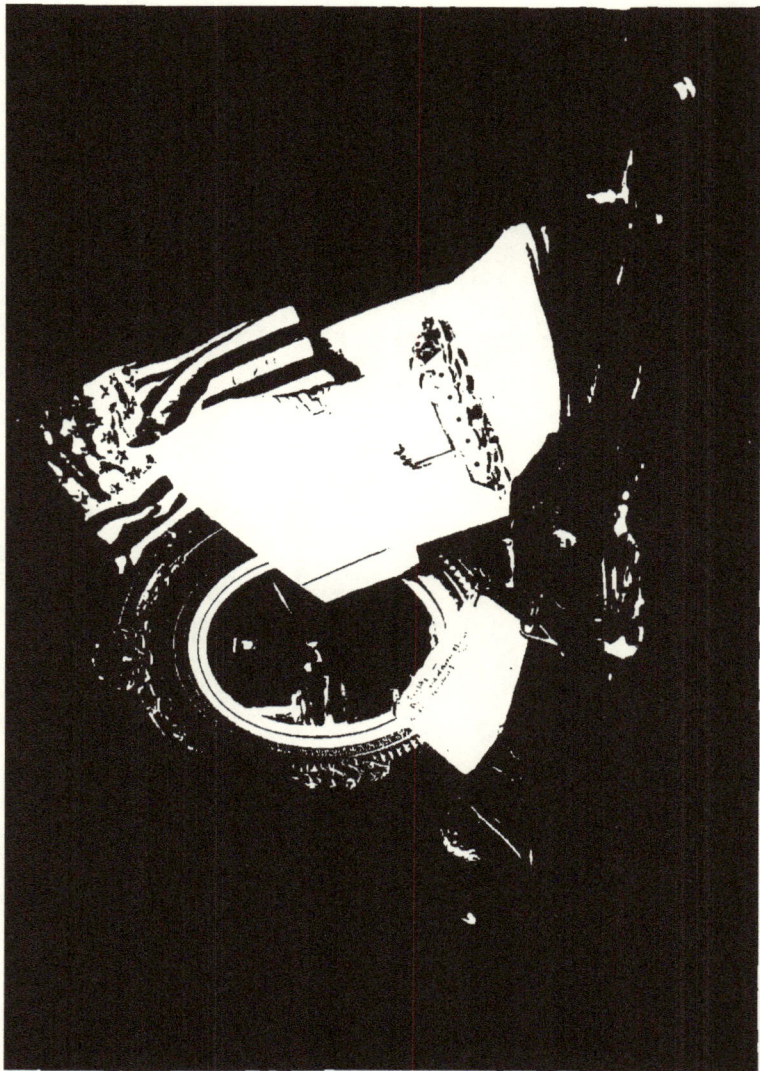

GORHAM C. TAYLOR and his Trophy—The Rebel Officer's Sword.

highest terms, for his daring adventure, and upon its successful termination, playfully remarking, "Why didn't you board that ram, and capture and bring *her* in, too? it would have made your fortune!" TAYLOR replied that that was hardly practicable with only six men. "Why, yes it was," said the Captain, "she has but sixty men, and *you and your six* could have boarded and carried her, sure!"

When the fleet had come to anchor, TAYLOR was directed to report the surrender to the Commander-in-Chief, and accordingly repaired on board the Flag-ship, and reported to Flag-officer FARRAGUT the surrender of the *Resolute*, and the bringing off her Commander, and at the same time delivered to him the sword. The Flag-officer inquired minutely into the particulars, and seemed much interested in the affair; asked who commanded the boat. "*I did, sir,*" said TAYLOR. "Why," said he, "you are a gallant fellow;" extolled his exploit, and complimented him highly, shaking his hand very warmly and cordially, and inquired his name, adding, "Take this sword, sir, and keep it as a trophy of your bravery, *and· a memorial of* THIS GLORIOUS DAY!" All of which was, of course, not a little gratifying to a young and ardent spirit that had gone· forth so gallantly in search of

" The bubble reputation."

"STATE OF NEW YORK,
"BUREAU OF MILITARY RECORD.

"Extract from a letter from Acting Master's Mate
"HOWARD T. MOFFAT, U. S. N.

"APRIL 25th, 1862.

"During the passage of the forts yesterday, one of the most
"gallant incidents was the capture of the *Resolute.* (rebel) by
"the *Sciota.* Master's Mate TAYLOR, of the latter, boarded
"the *Resolute,* in an open boat, under the hot fire, and received
"the sword of its Commander, which the Flag-officer presented
"to him for his conspicuous gallantry and bravery."

But, alas! for the sequel. This was the first, and believed
to be *the only Naval sword surrendered* on that glorious occasion; and the feat of the young officer was not surpassed, in
personal gallantry and heroism, by any individual act on that
day; and yet, in all the reports, all that appears of it is in
Fleet-Captain BELL's report, who, in speaking of the Captain of
the *Sciota,* * says he *"sent a boat's crew to take possession of
an armed steamer which surrendered to him!"* *That,* POSI-
TIVELY, IS ALL!! notwithstanding Captain BELL was know-
ing to all the particulars!!! But then, the hero of the exploit
was *only a "Volunteer!"*—albeit a son of the Empire State, of
good character and repute, qualified by ten years' experience
at sea, through all the grades of the merchant service, for any
position on any ship; whilst his grudging Commander was a
"Regular," or fossil of the old fogy, swallow-tailed pattern!

* If Captain DONALDSON, of the *Sciota,* made any report, himself, at all, it is not
published with the others.

It has been said that *every* "*regular*" officer received honorable mention, and most, if not all of them, promotion!

Strong must have been the confidence of the authorities in the deep-rooted patriotism and devotion to the sacred cause of the country, that permitted them to thus trifle with the aspirations for distinction and renown of the gallant fellows who rushed forward

" In the battle-path of duty,"

in that "dark and trying hour," and treat their gallant and chivalric services with neglect, contumely and scorn! Ah, well! thus wags the world!

The next day, the fleet, in its progress up the river, attacked and silenced extensive batteries at Chalmette, just below New Orleans. The *Sciota* took the *inside track*, rushing in to "short range," and bore a most conspicuous share in the action. There had been a large force actively working on the rebel fortifications, which extended for a mile or more on the bank of the river ; and, in clearing up on the approach of the fleet, great quantities of tools and implements, and wheelbarrows, were piled up as high as they could be thrown, like a great hay-stack. A 24-pounder shell, from one of TAYLOR'S howitzers, struck the stack, exploding in the center of it, and sent the wheelbarrows *kiting ;* some high in the air, and scattering fragments in every direction, and made a tremendous *splutter* generally, which raised great shouts and laughter throughout half a dozen of the nearest vessels of the fleet. "See the wheelbarrows!—ha! ha! Hey, the wheelbarrows!

Ho!—give 'em another!" with like shouts and cheers, was heard in every direction from the vessels near them.

The fleet anchored in front of the city, their guns trained on some of the most important points, ready to open fire in a moment, should needs be. The authorities and the people, feeling the heel of the proud and victorious Northmen on their necks, were in no very complaisant mood, and had to be sharply dealt with.

The *Sciota* proceeded, in a day or two, on up the river, in the van of the operations in that direction, and was constantly engaged, during the whole summer, in cruising up and down the river, scouting, skirmishing and fighting, and occasionally shaking up the rebel population on its borders. The boys had a varied and sometimes amusing experience in the diversified adventures they encountered in trading with the "contrabands" for chickens, eggs and other luxuries; and in disciplining and rattling the seceshers, sometimes including the women, on the banks of the river.

.One day, as they were running up, a party of ladies, in front of a stately mansion on the bank of the river, made themselves very conspicuous by waving a rebel flag over their heads when the *Sciota* was in front of them. A boat was sent ashore and brought the party, including the head of the family, on board. The fair *Rebs* were greatly exercised at the dilemma in which they found themselves, and vehemently protested that it was only a party-colored net shawl, or "Nubia," that they were waving *in compliment to the boat*, and a great deal of that sort of *bosh;* but the Quarter-master was too *old a salt* to be beguiled by such nonsense, and maintained that it was a veritable rebel flag—that he could not be mistaken, as he had his glass on it the whole time ; which seemed to take the starch out of the lady *seceshers.* The Captain gave them the assurance that wherever *that flag* should wave, in his presence, whether in the hands of men or women, *he should fire upon it.* He then dismissed them with a respectful but decisive reproof.

At another time, they were passing a large nunnery estab-lishment, a "full regulation" affair, standing a little way back from the river, a short distance above New Orleans—a *French* flag was hoisted on it. A boat was sent with a message to the Lady *head man*, directing that the flag be taken down, and that nothing but the national flag should fly in sight from the river. *Madame* was highly incensed at the *insulting order*, and complied, with a good deal of grimace and evidence of bad feeling. A few days afterward, in passing the establish-ment, the same flag was again flaunted in their faces, when the Captain sent a party to bring it off, which was done in short order. The boys were marched into the house without parley, and up to the top of it, and secured the flag *sans ceremonie*, to the great horror of the inmates at the sacrilegious outrage and desecration of their immaculate establishment, into which a *man's* foot never had, and they pretended never was to, enter. They made a terrible hellibaloo and sputtering about it ; but the only satisfaction they got was the assurance that if the in-terdicted flag was again displayed, it would be fired upon at sight, without parley or notice.

They participated in knocking and burning Grand Gulf, and smashing Natchez, some. When the affair at Baton Rouge came off, the *Sciota* happened to be at New Orleans *en dishabille*, her engine being overhauled. On getting the order, she pushed up, as soon as possible, *in double quick*, but was just too late for a chance in, and her share in pounding to death her quondam acquaintance, the ram *Arkansas*. She had a prominent part in the attack, on the 28th June, on the batteries at Vicksburg, driving their garrison out, and after a severe fight, passing by them, up.

In the forepart of July, Captain DONALDSON's health being much impaired, he retired from the command, and was succeeded by Lieutenant-Commander LOWRY, late First of the *Brooklyn.*

Whilst lying quietly at anchor near the mouth of the Yazoo, above Vicksburg, on the morning of the fifteenth of July, they were attacked by, and had a sharp conflict with, the new rebel iron-clad ram *Arkansas*, as she ran through the fleet, downwards; and then, on the same day, they attacked her in turn, and the batteries of Vicksburg, under which, being badly crippled in the morning's fight, she had taken shelter; and, after giving them a good hammering, run by them, down.

They were daily, and almost hourly, fired at by, and skirmishing with, Guerillas laying in the *brake* on the shores of the river. TAYLOR, having the howitzers, it was frequently his duty to throw a few rounds of grape or shrapnel, and occasionally a shell, pointing at where the whiffs of white smoke puffed up from the dense thickets, to disperse the annoyance.

One day in the latter part of September, as the *Sciota*, with two other boats, was running quietly up the river, scouting for adventure—being close under the east bank, some sixty or seventy miles up from New Orleans—a large drove of cattle was discovered on the shore; it had been swum across the river a short distance above, on its way from Texas, bound for the rebel camps in the vicinity; a hint, in the shape of a cannon shot from the *Sciota*, was given to the conductors of the drove, to "heave to," as others, as well as Johnny Reb, might have an appetite for fresh beef. After considerable effort to scatter and stampede their charge, they concluded, under the running fire of musketry directed at them, to give it up. Details from the gunboats were landed to take charge of the cattle. The drove was found to consist of sixteen hundred head; they were driven to an adjacent plantation on the bank of the river, and *corralled;* and the conductors placed in confinement in a church hard by, to the great annoyance and disgust of the good *padre* in charge of it; he, evidently, not deeming a company of wild Texan cattle drivers a very interesting or creditable congregation. TAYLOR and another officer were sent in command of the details from the *Sciota*, for the guarding of the *corral*, and keeping up night and day pickets, to prevent a surprise and stampede. They found the service anything but agreeable, being amongst a hostile population, and without any knowledge of what might be near them, or how soon they might be rushed upon by Guerrillas from the high cane with which the country was covered. Many amusing, and some

perilous incidents occurred, from the scouts and sentinels mis-
taking each other in the night for enemies, and in dealing with
the darkies for chickens and turkeys, and such other dainties as
could be had. They were thus employed for five or six days
and nights, until the arrival of steamers from New Orleans,
that were sent for, to convey the cattle down. After they were
embarked on the transport steamers, they all started down the
river. As they approached Donaldsonville, on the 4th of October, a large crowd of women and children were seen gathered
on the Levee, and the Captain came to the conclusion at once,
that there was trouble a-brewing. "There could not," he said,
"be such a gathering of women without mischief coming out of
it!" The *Sciota* was on the lead, and as she came abreast of
them, sure enough, the women suddenly *skedaddled* to the
rear, and five or six regiments of rebs, numbering upwards of
2000, with six pieces of artillery, which had all been completely
masked by the women, suddenly rose up on the Levee, and
opened a terrific fire at not over fifty yards distance. The
Sciota, being in advance, received the brunt of the fire of the
whole body. Lieutenant Swasey, her first Lieutenant, was
killed by a 6-pounder shot. The fire was returned with strik-
ing effect. The *Sciota* rounding to, to make a clean thing of it,
had driven the Johnnies to cover, and out of range by the time
the other boats, which were the rear-guard of the transports,
got in for a share in the scrimmage. When Donaldsonville
was taken possession of, a short time afterward, *one hundred
and eighty odd* new graves were counted in the church-yard,
inscribed with the names of men who had *died on the 4th of
October!*—very suggestive of the effect of the fire from the
Sciota ; not the least telling of which was the grape and can-

nister liberally furnished from TAYLOR's howitzers; and there must have been very many wounded in addition.

It was said, when the *Sciota* returned to New Orleans, that she had passed through harder service, and received more hits and knocks than any other vessel of the fleet.

In January, 1863, TAYLOR was ordered to New York, and on his arrival, and reporting to the Department, he was, on the report of an Examining Board of Navy Surgeons, previously held at New Orleans, *invalided* out, as being below the technical standard for robustness, notwithstanding he had served for nearly a year and a half in all the most severe and trying duties, and in the deadly climate of the Mississippi River, in the summer season; and was, in fact, the *only officer in his ship* who was never, during the whole time, on the sick list, or lost a day from duty; but being *only a volunteer*, of course he received no sign of recognition or appreciation of his services. During the whole term he filled the position and performed the *duty* of a Lieutenant, being a regular Deck-officer, and commanding a Division, &c., with only the rating of a *Master's Mate!*

When he was about to leave the *Sciota* for the Government transport, to proceed to New York, his "traps" were in one of the ship's boats, and he stepped into the cabin to take leave of the Captain, who inquired if he was ready to start, and was informed that his things were in the boat waiting alongside; he told him to hold on a moment, and he would give him a letter.

TAYLOR returned to the deck, and in a few minutes the Captain came up and handed him the following :

"U. S. GUNBOAT SCIOTA,

"NEW ORLEANS, La., Jan. 2, 186❡

"SIR : It gives me great pleasure, in parting with you, to "testify to your uniform good conduct, zeal and courage while "under my command. I hope that on the restoration of your "health, you will be ordered to some service which will again "give you an opportunity to serve your country as faithfully "as you have done on board of this vessel.

"I am, yours very truly,

"R. B. LOWRY,

"*Lt.-Com. U. S. Navy.*

"To Acting Master's Mate,

"G. C. TAYLOR,

"*U. S. Navy.*"

The Captain, observing that it was "a cutter" that was in waiting, ordered it up, and directed his GIG "Called away" for the occasion ; and, as they pulled off from the ship, the crew rushed to the sides and rigging at the call to "Cheer ship," and gave three cheers for Mr. TAYLOR, with an earnestness and enthusiasm indicating the deep feelings of interest and respect that prompted the movement. The boat's crew laid on their oars whilst the cheers were given. TAYLOR, standing in the stern sheets, raised his cap in token of acknowledgment and

29

appreciation of the compliment of the warm-hearted fellows—companions in so many battles and perils that they had gone through together, fighting in the cause of the Constitution and Government of their country, and in support of its glorious old flag,

" Proud banner of the free!
" The sky-born stars, and glorious colors three ! "

JULY, 1868.

HE NOW SLEEPS, CALMLY AND SWEETLY,
" THE BRIGHT-DREAMED SLUMBER OF THE BRAVE,"
WHERE WE LAID HIM, AMIDST HIS ANCESTRAL
" KITH AND KIN," BENEATH THE SOIL OF FAIRVIEW
CEMETERY, MIDDLETOWN, NEW JERSEY.

When GORHAM lay over at San Francisco in '59 and '60, Mr.
B——, a young gentleman, a civil engineer, engaged in the construction of a railroad, who was a cousin to his Aunt Fannie, was
domiciled with him at his Uncle Edward Taylor's. A warm friendship grew up between them; GORHAM often spoke of his friend,
"Gus" B——, in the warmest terms. I sent him a copy of the
little book on GORHAM'S SERVICES; this is the response.—A. T.

Office of the
Pacific and Sacramento Valley Railroad Company,

Shingle Springs, Cal., Aug. 23d, 1869.

To Asher Taylor, Esq.,

New York,

My Dear Sir :

Your sister, Mrs. Edward
Taylor, lately handed me a book from you, inscribed—"Gor-
ham's Friend." I take the earliest opportunity of expressing
not only my thanks for the remembrance, but for the honor you
do me. I now feel that in meeting you, which I sometime
hope to do, that I would not be a stranger.

My acquaintance with Gorham began in your brother's
house, where we shared bed and board together for several
months. I need not say that the acquaintance ripened into a
warm friendship, for the compliment you have paid me shows
that my name must have often been on his lips, while his
memory with me has been gratefully cherished.

Those winter hours we passed together in San Francisco
possessed a charm to me not easily described. His wit and

shrewd sayings, anecdotes, tales of voyages, and descriptions of
the various people, ports, climes, and seas, which he had visited,
all spiced with the romance of a true sailor, was to me an in-
describable pleasure. And I wish to testify—though it can add
nothing to a memory already precious to you—that all his sen-
timents, expressed either in public or private, were noble
and manly, as became a fearless and honest gentleman.

On his departure for the South Pacific, I saw him for the
last time; just before he sailed I spent several hours with him
on board of the little vessel. He was greatly pleased with the
prospective voyage, and his hopeful and unselfish spirit beat
high as his imagination conjured up fabulous returns for the
owners. Little did either of us think of the coming struggle in
which he was to take such an active and perilous part. I have
always deeply regretted that I did not see him again on his
return to San Francisco.

After the breaking out of the rebellion, I learned through
his Uncle Edward of his entering the navy. In August, 1862,
I received a letter from him dated U. S. Gunboat Sciota, off
Grand Gulf, Miss., June 13th. Of the pride and pleasure that
letter gave me, I cannot tell, and I turn to it now with increased
satisfaction.

The letter briefly and modestly described his participation
in the glorious passage of the fleet to New Orleans, promising
a fuller account at some future time. He says—"they have

just received orders from the commander to ' take·Vicksburg,' and push on to Memphis ; it is a big pill, but we can swallow it. The navy never stops. When they have once started to do a thing, they generally manage to get through somehow." He also says—"I expect at this time to-morrow evening we shall be hotly engaged by the fortifications at Vicksburg."

This cool-headed and brave-hearted sailor-patriot doubly endeared himself to me, and I esteem it no small honor to have been intimate with him. To such as he, serving both on flood and field, America owes her life and greatness.

·Our brave volunteers, whose deeds too often were obscured by the jealousies of the " regulars," gave the nation its victories ; saved those who loved the country and the flag, the humiliation of defeat, disintegration, and the annihilation of our republican form of government.

The last letter I received from your son, was at the time of his marriage, in which were enclosed cartes of himself and wife. I responded, but presume that multiplicity of business and ill-health prevented further correspondence on his part.

Next was the sad news of his decease; a blow keenly felt by us here who knew him, but a parent alone can suffer the sharp sorrow of such affliction. Through the son, I know how closely and warmly the tendrils of your heart wound about him ; of. the affectionate and tender regard which followed him from sea to sea, from shore to shore ; and I can imagine the great *wealth of love which went out from your soul when placing him in his final abiding-place.*

While it is true that in the process of nature we are taught, and expect to depart before our children, yet the reverse is often the case. We must mourn, and be mourned; and it is beyond human power to entirely remove the bitter pains.

But I know and rejoice, that for you there are proud recollections which bring consolation, if not relief.

> *"The good knights are dust,*
> *Their good sword's are rust;*
> *Their souls are with the saints, I trust."**

At the coming anniversary of his burial, when you strew his tomb with flowers, I beg that for me you will place at his feet a bunch of blue violets, a small token of my friendship and respect.

I remain sir,

Your very obedient servant

F. A. B.

---

*Probably quoted from memory; right reading:

> *"The knight's bones are dust,*
> *And his good sword rust;*
> *His soul is with the saints, I trust."*
>
> COLERIDGE—*"The Knight's Tomb."*